COUNT ME IN

CAL RIPKEN JR.

with Greg Brown

Illustrations by Doug Keith

TAYLOR PUBLISHING
Dallas, Texas

Greg Brown lives in Bothell, Washington, with his wife Stacy and two children. The co-author of the best-selling children's book *Things Change* with Troy Aikman, he also co-authored *Kirby Puckett: Be the Best You Can Be* and *Edgar Martinez: Patience Pays*.

Doug Keith provided the illustrations for Troy Aikman's best-selling children's book, *Things Change*. His illustrations have appeared in national magazines, greeting cards, and books, and major sports teams have used his work in their promotional advertising.

Published by Taylor Publishing
    1550 West Mockingbird Lane
    Dallas, Texas 75235

Library of Congress Cataloging-in-Publication Data

Ripken, Cal, 1960–
        Count me in / Cal Ripken with Greg Brown ; illustrations by Doug
Keith.
            p.   cm.
        Summary: An autobiography of the superstar shortstop for the
Baltimore Orioles baseball team.
        ISBN 0-87833-915-9
        1. Ripken, Cal, 1960–   —Juvenile literature. 2. Baseball
players—United States—Biography—Juvenile literature.
3. Baltimore Orioles—Juvenile literature. [1. Ripken, Cal, 1960–.
2. Baseball players.] I. Brown, Greg. II. Keith, Doug, ill.
III. Title.
GV865.R47A3   1995
796.357'092—dc20
[B]   95-31921
                                                        CIP
                                                        AC

Printed in the United States of America

10   9   8   7   6   5   4   3   2

*Cal Ripken, Jr. has donated all of his proceeds from the sale of this book to the **Kelly & Cal Ripken, Jr. Foundation**, a non-profit organization founded by Cal and his wife, Kelly, to support literacy, health, and community service programs.*

Cal at age 5

My name is Cal Ripken, Jr., and I play shortstop for the Baltimore Orioles.

Playing baseball has taught me many great lessons about the game of life. I have written this book to share with you some of what I've learned so you can find success on whatever road you travel.

Focus on Sports (bat rack), Scott Wachter (Cal as adult), Ripken Family (Cal at 5)

I've played in thousands of games during my career, but I still remember sitting on the bench my first season in the majors.

I ate so many sunflower seeds waiting for my turn to play, I thought my destiny would be to collect a record number of shells.

Not being counted in made my insides ache. Each frustrating day I sat and munched those salty seeds, I promised myself: "When I get my chance to play, I'm not coming out."

Focus on Sports

National Baseball Library, Cooperstown, NY

Lou Gehrig (1903–41) played for the New York Yankees from 1925 to 1939 as a first baseman. A teammate with Babe Ruth, Gehrig had a lifetime batting average of .340 and played in seven World Series. People called Gehrig "The Iron Horse" because of his consecutive games record. But a rare disease ended his streak and later cut short his life at age 37.

On May 30, 1982, I became a full-time starter for the Orioles. For that season and the next 12, I did not miss playing in an Orioles game. Playing in so many consecutive games became known as "The Streak."

Going into the 1995 season, I had a chance to break Lou Gehrig's record of playing in 2,130 consecutive games. I needed to play in just 122 more games to break a record many thought would last forever.

Some have called me an "Iron Man" because of "The Streak."

I suppose there would be advantages to being a real iron man. I'd be super strong, tough, fearless, never tire and never feel pain.

Of course, I'm human, just like you. Sometimes I feel weak. Sometimes I'm afraid. Sometimes I tire. Sometimes I hurt.

Just because I've played in many major league games, I am not a baseball machine.

Baseball has been a way of life for me for a long time. But it is not my whole life. To understand this, we have to look back to my childhood.

Ripken Family

Ripken Family

I was born into a baseball family on August 24, 1960, in Havre de Grace, Maryland, and named Calvin Edwin Ripken, Junior.

My father, whose name is also Cal Ripken, missed my birth because he was playing professional baseball in the minor leagues.

My mother loved the game, too. She played softball in high school, and my parents met at one of her games.

I'm the second of four children. My sister, Elly, is one and a half years older, brother Fred is one year younger, and brother Billy is four years younger.

Jay Spencer / Miami News

Ripken Family

My father played catcher in the minors six years until a foul ball hit him in the shoulder. The injury ended his playing career when I was about one year old.

Dad, however, stayed in baseball as a coach and manager.

Because of his job, our lives revolved around baseball.

We'd go to his games and watch from the stands. I'd sing along with fans at the start of the game and during the seventh-inning stretch. On special days, we'd go onto the field for a picture.

Ripken Family

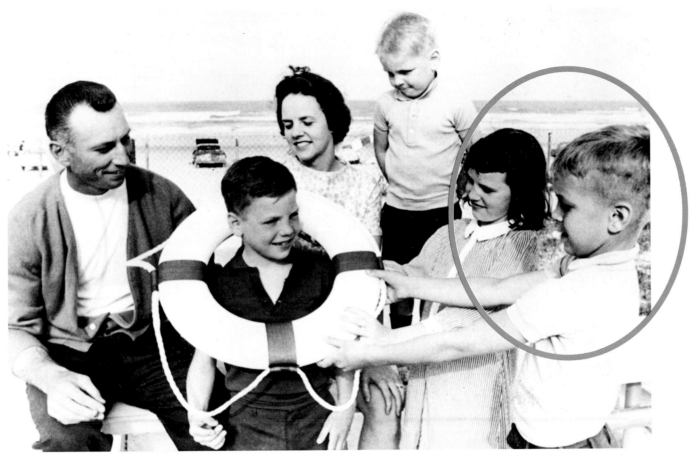

Ripken Family

We didn't spend all our time at baseball parks, although it seemed we did. As we traveled around the country, my parents took us to special places, including this trip to a beach when I was seven.

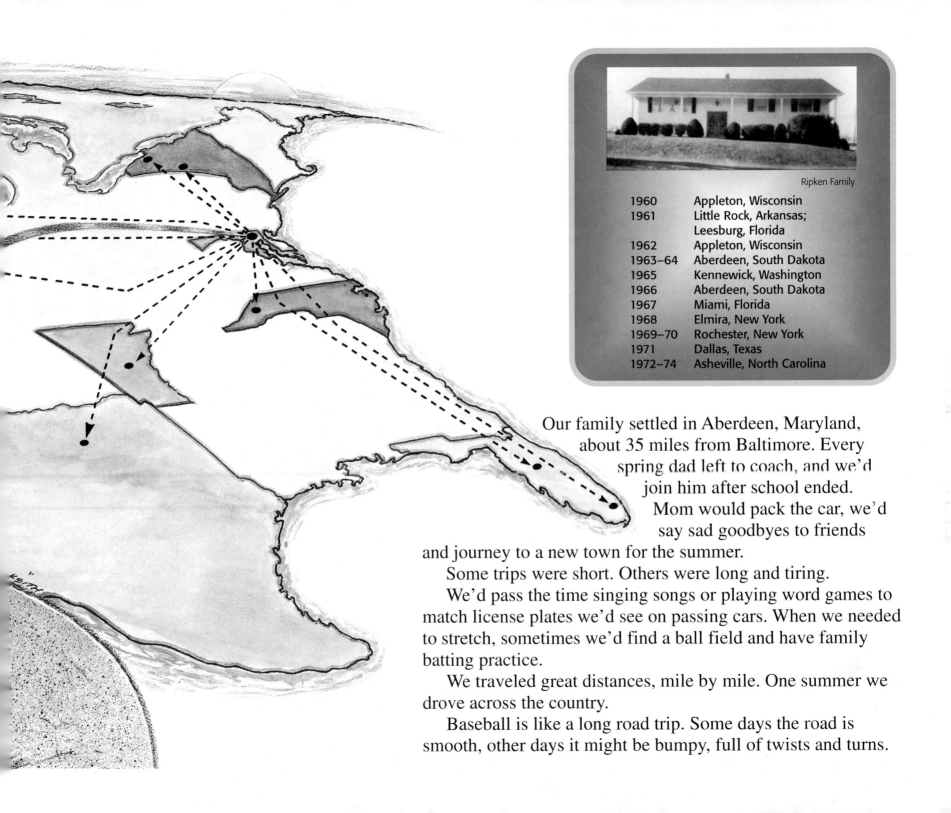

Ripken Family

1960	Appleton, Wisconsin
1961	Little Rock, Arkansas; Leesburg, Florida
1962	Appleton, Wisconsin
1963–64	Aberdeen, South Dakota
1965	Kennewick, Washington
1966	Aberdeen, South Dakota
1967	Miami, Florida
1968	Elmira, New York
1969–70	Rochester, New York
1971	Dallas, Texas
1972–74	Asheville, North Carolina

Our family settled in Aberdeen, Maryland, about 35 miles from Baltimore. Every spring dad left to coach, and we'd join him after school ended.

Mom would pack the car, we'd say sad goodbyes to friends and journey to a new town for the summer.

Some trips were short. Others were long and tiring.

We'd pass the time singing songs or playing word games to match license plates we'd see on passing cars. When we needed to stretch, sometimes we'd find a ball field and have family batting practice.

We traveled great distances, mile by mile. One summer we drove across the country.

Baseball is like a long road trip. Some days the road is smooth, other days it might be bumpy, full of twists and turns.

Because of our strong family love, no matter where we were we felt secure and stable.

More than anything, we loved playing games and sports together. We'd play board games, cards, ping-pong, backyard volleyball, bowling, soccer or baseball.

We all loved playing; however, I mostly loved winning.

Everything had to be a competition. I had to win. Mom would say, "Come on Calvin, it's just for fun."

To me, it wasn't fun unless I won.

Looking back, I'm surprised anybody played with me because I was such a poor sport. If I won, I'd brag by celebrating in the loser's face. If I lost, I'd pout or whine or keep playing until I won.

Often when we'd play cards someone would yell: "Mom, Cal's cheating again!"

"Am not."

"Are too!"

"Am not."

I was cheating, but I wouldn't admit it. I put winning ahead of everything, even the people I loved.

When I was seven, I remember teaching the girl next door how to play checkers. I explained the rules, and we started playing on our porch. I'd give her hints with my eyes where to move. Secretly, I schemed against her.

My plan worked as I jumped five in a row to win.

I sprang to my feet and threw my head back in wild celebration, forgetting a window sill above.

A sharp pain bolted through me as my head cracked into the concrete. I needed five stitches.

This was a come-to-my-senses call. Cheating is like taking a shortcut, and there are no shortcuts to success. Cheating only cheats yourself.

Because I didn't attend kindergarten, my first experience with school came in the first grade that fall in Aberdeen.

My only trouble throughout school came during the first two weeks.

I had trouble sitting still. Whenever the teacher turned around, I'd grab my books and coat and run out of class and down the hall to go home. Each time, my teacher, or another school official, stopped me from leaving. There was talk of holding me back.

Finally I settled down and enjoyed my years in school. I finished high school with a B+ grade average. Math was my favorite subject.

Ripken Family

Scott Wachter

Harry Connolly

When I wasn't thinking about school, baseball filled my thoughts.

I still remember my first Little League game. Our team, the Angels, played on a huge lot behind a school. I thought it was the best field in the world. To us, it seemed as great as the major leagues.

Baseball captured my imagination. My parents took us to see the Baltimore Orioles win a World Series game when I was 6. They bought me a pennant that lived on my wall and a bobbing head mascot doll that stood on my dresser for years.

As my love for the game grew, so did my list of questions. I took full advantage of my dad's job. I'd go to his minor league games and shag fly balls in the outfield during pregame practices.

During games our whole family helped. I'd be batboy, my brothers would help in the clubhouse and Elly chipped in scorekeeping.

I found myself constantly asking players questions about baseball fundamentals, rules and strategy. Then I'd check with Dad for his views about what they said.

Asking questions is one of the best ways to learn.

Ripken Family

One question I had a tough time understanding: "Why was Dad away from home so often?"

Deep inside, I knew the answer. Yet, it hurt. Baseball took my dad away from me.

I noticed his absence most at my games. All my other teammates' dads attended the games. My dad watched only a handful of my games from Little League through high school.

Mom, however, always managed to support me at the games from her lawn chair. She gave me tips on batting and fielding. During the games that Dad watched, I usually tried too hard to impress him and didn't play well.

I figured I'd have to make the best of the time Dad and I did share. On Saturday mornings, I'd go with Dad to his baseball clinics at the stadium. There, I'd sit in the sun listening to Dad repeat baseball tips I had heard many times.

Our time, however, came during the 30-minute drive to and from the ballpark. I'd fire off questions, and often we'd have long talks in the car. He'd tell me baseball stories from his playing days and the toughness of his old teammates. Being together is what counted.

Dad did attend my final Little League game. The summer of 1972 we lived in Asheville, North Carolina, and I made the league's all-star team.

We won our state tournament and advanced to the regional playoffs in St. Petersburg, Florida. We won our first game 8–5.

I pitched the second game. Two more wins would send us to the World Series in Williamsport, Pennsylvania.

Unfortunately, I surrendered a home run late in the game, and we lost to a team from Kentucky.

Heartbroken, our team cried a river of tears.

I faced plenty of setbacks my early years. I made mistakes that lost games. Coaches pulled me from the pitching mound when I lost my control or tired.

Often I needed my parents to wrap their arms around me and squeeze confidence into me.

Ripken Family

I'm grateful those defeats didn't destroy my desire for playing baseball.

I moved on to play in the summer Babe Ruth and Mickey Mantle leagues.

During the fall, I tried youth-league soccer. Later, I played soccer in high school and earned two letters, became team captain, and made two all-star teams. Baseball, however, remained number one in my heart.

Ripken Family

Ripken Family

My freshman year in high school I stood
5-foot-7 and weighed 128 pounds. Despite my small
size, lack of returning veterans helped me win the
job at second base. I quickly learned baseball can be
rough when a 6-foot-5 inch, 200-pound opponent
crashed into me at second base.

He knocked me off my feet with a blow to my
ribs. I gasped for air as Coach Don Morrison
checked on me.

"Please don't take me out," I pleaded.

Coach Morrison did take me out, but I re-entered
the game a few innings later.

I showed good hands fielding, yet struggled at the
plate, hitting below my weight. I batted last in the
line up and bunted my share of the time.

The next season, I grew a few more inches and
added some weight. Coach switched me to shortstop.

Scouts noticed me pitching my junior year for the Aberdeen Eagles. I stood 6 feet tall and started to throw the ball with some pop. Our summer team in the Mickey Mantle League went all the way to the World Series, only to lose.

Ripken Family

By then, Dad worked for the Orioles' big league team as a coach. That allowed me access to major league pitchers, and I continued to ask questions. I developed an 86-mph fastball and learned a curve, slider and change-up.

I grew two more inches and weighed 185 pounds my senior year in high school. Everything started coming together on the field. I won the county batting title with a .492 average while playing shortstop. I finished with a 7–2 pitching record; the best win being my last game.

I struck out 17 batters in our 7–2 win in the Class AAA Maryland high school championships against Thomas Stone High.

Ripken Family

A few days before the final high school game, the Orioles chose me with their fourth pick (second round, 44th overall) in the 1978 baseball draft. Some in the Baltimore organization thought I should pitch; others wanted me as an infielder.

They left the decision to me. I wanted to play every day, so I signed for $20,000 and $500 a month and went to rookie camp as a shortstop.

The first month in pro baseball I doubted my decision. My first day of practice I remember taking grounders behind Bob Bonner, a college player picked behind me out of Texas A&M.

The height of his skill level and maturity awed me.

"I'm never going to play if everybody plays this well," I told myself.

They promoted Bonner to Class AA, the middle of the O's minor league system. I, however, started at the bottom. My first taste of professional baseball began in rookie ball level at Bluefield, West Virginia.

I got my chance to play in Bluefield, but I made so many errors in the first two weeks that I feared I would be released from the team. I made two or three errors a game. Some mistakes cost us a win.

Returning to the ballpark each day took all my will power. Some Bluefield fans got on me, yelling "Go back to Little League!" I hoped the ball wouldn't be hit my way.

I had come to a crossroad in my life. I felt my confidence crumbling. After those rough games, sometimes I'd call home.

"I don't know how I'm going to make it," I told my parents. "I don't know how."

Mom and Dad had always pumped me back up.

"Always remember that no matter what happens on the field, you deserve to be there," Dad once said. "They've placed you in that position for a reason. You belong. Always believe that you belong."

Ripken Family

UPI/Bettman

I carried Dad's words on the field with me every night as I rebuilt my confidence. I finished my first season strong with a .264 batting average, although I did not hit a home run.

I played Class A at Miami in 1979. The team switched me to third base for half the season. In 1980, I played AA at Charlotte, North Carolina, where I began playing every day.

The O's promoted me to AAA in Rochester, New York, in 1981. Playing mostly at third, I filled in at shortstop for Bob Bonner, the player I admired my rookie year. That year I participated in baseball history, playing in the longest game ever—33 innings—at Pawtucket, Rhode Island. The April 18 game lasted 8 hours, 7 minutes before being postponed at 4:07 in the morning. We continued it two months later. Pawtucket won 3-2.

Staying alert mentally in a long game takes concentration. When faced with this situation, I talk to myself.

"C'mon! Let's go. Get yourself in gear. Where's the play? What's the count? Where does this guy hit off this pitcher?"

Such self-talk keeps me in the game.

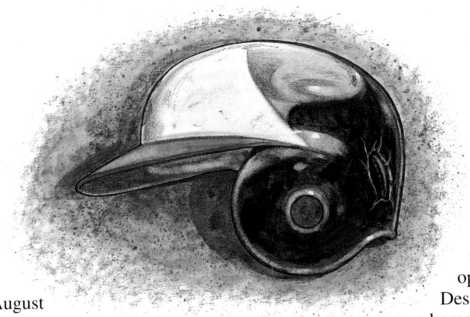

My dream of becoming a major-leaguer came true August 8, 1981, when the Orioles called me to Baltimore. Dad still coached third base.

The glow of being "in the show" didn't last long as I found myself sitting on the bench and rarely playing. In just 23 games, I hit .128.

That's when I promised myself not to come out once Manager Earl Weaver counted me in.

Opening Day of the 1982 season found me starting at third base. We opened against Kansas City. Despite being nervous, I belted a home run my first time at the plate. I finished with two more hits, making the game a highlight of my career. I started to believe I belonged.

That belief didn't last long as I fell into a terrible batting slump. I didn't snap out of it until a frightening fastball by Seattle's Mike Moore hit me in the head a month later. Thankfully, my helmet took most of the blow, leaving a lemon-sized hole.

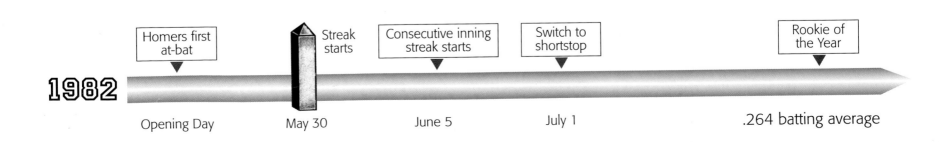

1982

| Homers first at-bat | Streak starts | Consecutive inning streak starts | Switch to shortstop | Rookie of the Year |

Opening Day | May 30 | June 5 | July 1 | .264 batting average

Michael Zagaris

Earl Weaver kept me out one game. Before facing Moore, my big-league batting average stood at .121.

As I pondered the effect of the beaning, determination surged through me.

I knew if I showed fear at the plate I would be finished with baseball. I couldn't let pitchers bully me. I had to go back in and show pitchers that high inside fastballs did not bother me. I hit .281 the rest of the season.

My 1982 season, however, is marked by a game we lost 6–0 to Toronto on May 30. This game started "The Streak."

That season also marked my shift from third base to shortstop. Weaver switched me even though at 6-foot-4 I'm the tallest ever to play the position regularly. He refused to listen to doubters who said I was not agile enough to play shortstop.

I refused to listen to those who didn't think I could succeed. Don't let what others say keep you from reaching your potential. Believe in your talents, and listen to your heart.

1983

First All-Star Game

Orioles win World Series

Major League Player of Year A.L. MVP

Focus on Sports

Focus on Sports

My dream came true in the 1983 season as our team played in the World Series against Philadelphia.

We won the Series in five games. The last out became special to me because I caught an easy line drive to end the season.

Squeezing that ball in my mitt burst a bubble of emotions. A season is long and difficult. To finally reach your goal is a rush of pure pride. Pride in how a group traveled a tough road together. Pride in proving to yourself you could go the distance.

Looking back, I didn't appreciate the moment. It came so early in my career, I expected to collect a handful of World Series rings.

As time has shown me, you can't always count on success being around every corner.

A.L. assist record
with 583

1984

All-Star

.304

Photo: Wide World Photos, Inc.

Teammate Eddie Murray guided me around some rough corners.

He counted me onto the team by offering his friendship. We all need friends to help us along the way.

At times I leaned on him, later he leaned on me.

I remember one night watching myself on TV throw a tantrum after striking out.

I vowed to try to control my temper even when anger burns like fireworks inside.

Then I noticed how Eddie reacted to strikeouts. He'd walk back calmly with his head held high. I learned how to be a professional watching Eddie.

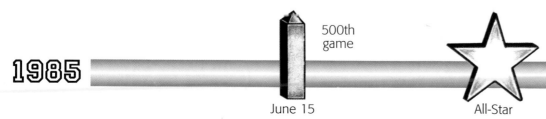

1985

500th game

June 15

All-Star

I also had the luxury of looking to Dad in the third-base coaches' box for advice.

Just as a coach gives players signals, Dad gave me signs of support in many ways.

He always tried to treat me like the rest of the players. A handshake became a sign—a way to say congratulations on a job well done, such as when rounding third base after hitting a home run.

Led A.L. shortstops in HRs 4th year in a row

1986

All-Star

.282

Focus on Sports

Our third-base ritual went on hold in the 1987 season when Dad became the manager.

In mid-summer our family made baseball history when my brother Billy joined the team and played second base. It was the first time a father managed two sons in the majors and the first time I played with Billy on the same team. The three of us together felt right and natural.

One of Dad's toughest calls came September 14th while losing 18–3 to Toronto.

"I'm going to take you out of the game. What do you think?" he said in the eighth inning.

"What do you think?" I asked.

"I think it's the right thing to do," Dad replied.

"OK then, I'll come out."

I sat, ending five years of playing every inning. My consecutive games streak stood intact as long as I played in part of a game.

Dad's managing career ended early in the 1988 season when our team lost its first six games. I heard about it on the radio driving to the ballpark. I walked into the clubhouse stunned, emotions whirling.

"You have a job to do," Dad told me later. "Do your job as best you can. I'll be fine."

Dad returned as third base coach, but five years later, the Orioles released Billy and Dad. I felt crushed. Dad retired. Billy signed on with the Texas Rangers.

| Dad becomes manager | Billy joins team |  | Consecutive innings streak ends at 8,243 | Marries Kelly |

1987

July 11

All-Star

September 14   November 13   .252

UPI/Bettman

The only thing I could do was swallow my frustration and pain and continue on. To keep going when the road turns uphill is a true test of character.

After the O's fired Dad, we set a major-league record by losing our first 21 games.

So I know all about winning and losing. To make it through, you need balance.

I don't know why, but I've always been able to balance the boy and man in me. There are times to be goofy and have fun and times to be serious and work hard.

A key to my longevity is preparation. I stick to a tough training schedule in the offseason. During the season, I eat good food, get plenty of sleep and practice before every game.

Working out often can be boring. I play games within games to make it fun. We'll have clubhouse contests—who can jump highest or farthest or play tape ball or hockey with brooms and baseballs. When taking infield in spring training, sometimes we'll put out cones as goalposts and challenge teammates to try and hit grounders between them while we try to field the ball.

A little creativity can help you keep your balance, too.

Scott Wachter

1988

Dad fired | O's 0–21

June 25 — 1,000th game

All-Star

.264

Having a life off the field keeps my balance.

Sports only goes so far to fill your heart.

Everybody needs the love of others to make life meaningful.

For me, that happened thanks to an autograph. One day, a woman kindly asked me to sign a paper napkin at a restaurant. She explained it was for her daughter.

I wrote: "Sorry I missed you if you are anything like your mother."

Months later, a 6-foot blonde walked up to me in a different restaurant and said, "Thanks for being so nice to my mom."

That's how I met Kelly in 1984. We dated, and on New Year's Eve 1986, I invited her to my house for a surprise that took me weeks to

prepare. It was a 6-foot by 8-foot sign made of plywood and Christmas lights.

When darkness fell, we went to the back sliding-glass door. I asked her to look into the backyard.

Then, with ring in hand, I flipped on the light switch to my sign: "Will you marry me?"

She said yes. We were married Nov. 13, 1987, a Friday.

1989

All-Star

Led O's in hits, 2Bs, RBIs

Rachel born—Nov. 22

Ripken family

Cisco Adler/York Daily Record

Kelly helped me over the years through Dad's firing, batting slumps, losing streaks and the criticism from some who thought "The Streak" hurt the team.

I do my best to be there when Kelly needs me. I even do chores around the house.

The births of my daughter, Rachel, and son, Ryan, gave me a new perspective on life.

Now I'm the one answering their questions of why baseball is taking me away. I explain it as best I can, but it's never easy leaving for road trips. I treasure the time we do spend together.

When I'm with Kelly and the kids, the pressures of baseball fade away, and I can refuel my energy.

Scott Wachter

1990

Moves to second in record book with 1,308th game in row

Sets M.L. fielding record with just 3 errors all season

June 12

All-Star

.250

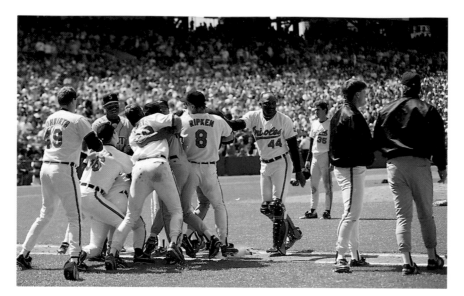
Scott Wachter

Even the most well-rested athletes experience bumps and bruises during a season. I've had my aches and pains along the way.

Three times during "The Streak" I suffered injuries that threatened to keep me out.

The most serious came June 6, 1993, while playing the Mariners. My spikes caught in the ground while being pushed during a shoving match, twisting my right knee. I played the rest of the game, but the next morning the knee swelled and felt stiff.

I woke up and told Kelly, "I don't think I can play today."

I could barely walk. I called my parents and told them about it. Before I knew it, they were over at my house. They didn't say much. We didn't talk about "The Streak," although it was on everyone's mind.

As the day continued, I tried walking around my driveway. Mom and Dad walked with me in silence.

"Hey, this is loosening up a little," I said as time came to leave for Camden Yards. Once there, we kept it hush-hush as I tested the knee.

Despite some discomfort, I knew I could play, and I made it through the game without a problem.

1991

Wide World Photos, Inc.

All-Star MVP

July 19

1,500th game

Gold Glove Award

34 homers, most by shortstop in 22 years

Major League Player of Year A.L. MVP

Many strange things can happen in baseball. Every game, the ball takes weird bounces, and there are freak accidents.

I could drive myself crazy thinking about all the odd ways I could be hurt playing baseball. More than 3,700 players were injured and put on the disabled list since "The Streak" began.

Despite the danger, I never worry about injuries. You can't live your life, or play your game, fearful of bad things that might happen.

Associated Press

Wide World Photos, Inc.

Wide World Photos, Inc.

1992

269th HR, most by O's right-hander

June 23

All-Star

1,000th RBI

August 31

Gold Glove Award

Wide World Photos, Inc.

.251

The 1994 season brought days of doubt. Labor differences between players and owners ended the season early and started 1995 late, hurting everyone, especially fans.

I never felt "The Streak" was more important than baseball. I would have sacrificed it to help other players. Thankfully, I did not need to make that choice.

Once we started playing again, I felt at peace about "The Streak."

Plenty of people worried for me as the record neared. However, I refused to think negatively. In every city we played, reporters asked the same questions over and over. That drained me mentally, but family and fans kept me going.

People everywhere reached out to me and gave me encouragement. Fans at home and on the road cheered me on. It felt as though every city was my hometown.

Such support helped me stay focused on the tasks of each day without looking too far ahead.

Scott Wachter

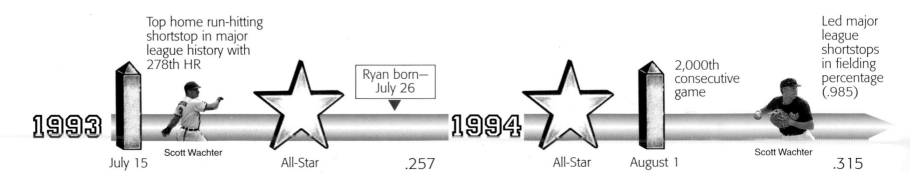

Top home run-hitting shortstop in major league history with 278th HR

Ryan born—
July 26

2,000th consecutive game

Led major league shortstops in fielding percentage (.985)

1993

Scott Wachter

July 15

All-Star

.257

1994

All-Star

August 1

Scott Wachter

.315

Months shrank to weeks; the weeks dwindled to days.

Huge numbers hung on the brick B&O Warehouse beyond rightfield to keep track of my games played.

Finally, on September 6, 1995, the people most important to me gathered together at Camden Yards with an overflow crowd of 48,262. Everyone showered me with unforgettable warmth.

I will always remember the way the night's drama magically unfolded. We defeated the California Angels 4–2, and I even hit a home run.

One Moment in Time

The game became official in the middle of the fifth inning, and the celebration began. As I ran into the dugout, fans stood and waves of applause poured down.

The numbers on the warehouse rolled down to mark my 2,131st straight game. Fireworks blasted off the stadium roof, and music stirred emotions. It was unbelievable.

I made my way to Kelly and our children and gave my hat and jersey to Rachel and Ryan, showing off a T-shirt Rachel had given me that morning. It said: "2130+ Hugs and Kisses for Daddy."

With much emotion I waved and tapped my heart to say thank you to fans. The standing ovation lasted more than 22 minutes, drawing me out of the dugout again and again.

Teammates pushed me onto the field for a victory lap. I circled the field, high fiving, hugging and shaking the hands of hundreds of fans.

Seeing the smiles, tears and excitement in their eyes made the night my special moment in time.

1995

July 4 — Orioles all-time runs leader

13th consecutive All-Star Game

September 6 — Sets major league record for consecutive games played with 2,131st game

Played in 99 percent of Orioles innings during streak

A ceremony after the game brought many special people onto the field. Gifts were given to me, and many nice things were said.

A treasured compliment came from Joe DiMaggio, who played with Lou Gehrig. He said, "Wherever [Gehrig] is, I'm sure he's tippin' his cap to you, Cal Ripken."

I thanked everyone as best I could, and the touching night came to an end. What made me most proud was how the night showed the world how special baseball can and should be.

To me, the game wasn't about breaking a record because I never set out to top Gehrig's mark. It just happened. It was really about playing the game I love the only way I know how—trying my best each day.

As you continue your road of life, remember that it takes commitment to succeed in anything—school, work and even relationships. To go anywhere, to achieve anything, it all starts by saying these three words each day: Count Me In.